The Mother's Companion To Woman In Love

Twelve Conversations

Every Mother Should Have With Her

Daughter

BY KATIE HARTFIEL

Hearts United Inc.

PO Box 6947
Katy, Texas 77491

www.womaninlove.org

Acknowledgements

Thanks be to God! Thank you to all the mothers who have inspired me in my own journey of motherhood! Thank you especially to those who contributed their gifts, time and insights to this Mother's Companion. Special thanks to TJ Burns, Shelley Garza, Abby and Rhonda Gruenewald, Rhonda and Sarah Grace Hunsucker, Connie Klenke and Cheri and Bernadette Mahoney. Additionally, I am extremely grateful to my mother-in-law, Sandra for her witness as a prayer warrior. Her prayers for her son and his future spouse were undoubtedly heard and for that I am both humbled and grateful!

Cover Design: Saint Louis Creative and TJ Burns

Table of Contents

Introduction:

"The Talk." Every parent dreads it. No child enjoys it. I will never forget when I discovered *the truth*. I was in fifth grade and, honestly, I had never thought to ask where babies came from. I knew it required a mother and a father and I figured the Lord just placed a baby in the womb when He saw fit. That was enough for me. One evening my mother asked if I would like to stay up past bedtime and watch a video with her. Heck yes! I couldn't believe my luck... of course I did! That was until I discovered the content and discussed my newfound knowledge with her. I didn't sleep well that evening as I lay on the top bunk of my room. The discomfort was enough to keep me from bringing the topic up again. I am sure this was much to my parent's relief!

As a youth minister, I often dealt with parents who complained about their teen's obligation to come to our parish for catechesis. It seemed that the one night that was met with zero grievances about attendance happened to be the evening dedicated to sexuality. Parents would often tell me how glad they were to send their child elsewhere to hear the message of chastity. While these expressions were disheartening I couldn't help but empathize! I am sure their teenage children felt the same way! The fact of the matter is that my job in youth ministry was always intended to be a support and supplement for the primary catechist of every child- the parent. The truth is that there is no better way to increase your child's chance of success in this area than to have **your** support and communication.

I hope this book will be your ticket to communication with your daughter. I hope you and I can approach her **together**. The premise of *Woman in Love* is based on hope. We have hope that the Lord created your daughter with an incredible vocation. You know her better than anyone and

He knows her even better than you do! If she is called to marriage, the Omnipotent Lord knows who she will marry. If this is true, then that young man is out there somewhere right now. *Woman in Love* aims to help your daughter hold out for true love. This *Mother's Companion* aims to help your daughter know she is truly loved, in her own home, **right now**.

I wrote *Woman in Love* with a desire to reach young women with a solid message that contrasts the world around them. The term "Woman in Love" was coined in my youth program as an alternative to the title, "Woman of God." We began to use it widely to express our passion for the Savior. When a woman is in love, she wants to shout it from the rooftops. Love changes her... love changed me... love changed you. The book aims to answer tough questions about purity, dating and sexuality while weaving in my personal story of falling in love with Christ and then my husband. It is the account of my conviction and life of prayer for the soul of my future spouse. As you will discover through the book, my prayers and the letters I began to write to my Husband-To-Be played an enormous role in the outcome of our relationship. God is so good and I know He is longing for the opportunity to write more and more love stories... including that of your baby girl.

There is however, more to my story than is recounted in *Woman in Love*. On the eve of my wedding, at the conclusion of our rehearsal, my then-fiancé's mother came and hugged me in the back of the church. As she did so, she said, "Girl, I have been praying for you since before you were born." Wow. Until that moment I didn't know that she had been praying for her son's future wife since he was born. Through every temptation, grace-filled encounter, trial, hardship and victory of my life this woman was praying for me every day. I know that the Lord heard and answered her prayers for her son and her prayers for me! Praise God for that!

In the pages that follow you will find tips on how to pray for and speak to your daughter concerning this tough topic. Furthermore, you will find some suggestions for chapter by chapter refection, prayer and discussion. Disclaimer: This booklet is meant to open the door for you as a mother. Mother/Daughter relationships are complex. The personality blends of women are complicated and each one is unique. This Mother's Companion is not meant to be an extensive manual for dialogue, but I hope it will be a solid starting point.

I would love to hear your experience of this journey. Please e-mail me with your glory stories, questions and suggestions. You can contact me through my webpage where you can also connect via facebook.

God bless you and know my prayers are with you,

Katie

Further Tips For Talking To Your Daughter About Sexuality

#1 Embrace the awkwardness!

Yes, sometimes this journey may be weird, uncomfortable and difficult! At times you will think, "I can't believe I'm talking about this with my baby." Although I have spoken to both large crowds and guided many through private conversations regarding this topic, the awkward train still tends to pull up to my station.

I have found two tricks that seem to help me. First off, I have found that sometimes pointing out the awkwardness is easier than trying to cover it up. Don't feel like you always have to play it cool. It's ok to say, "This is tough to talk about, but this is good for us." Acknowledge the elephant in the room and invite him into the conversation. Secondly, we know you are mature enough to handle these topics and you daughter does too. You don't have to prove it by keeping a straight face. Don't' be afraid to laugh together, sometimes giggling can be a great way to unleash some tension.

#2 Create a safe zone

Be sure your environment is conducive to no interruptions. No one wants their teenage brother walking in at a time like this! Find a time and space that works best for each of you. This may be at home, at a restaurant, at a park or even a space on your parish grounds.

Hopefully the suggested conversations in this book will lead to more conversations outside of your scheduled meet-up time or after you've completed this book. I would suggest setting up a "secret signal" so your daughter can let you know when they need some time alone to discuss something with you. A friend recommended presenting the daughter with a candle that you light during every conversation regarding *Woman in Love*. In the future, if there is something on her heart, tell her to bring that candle out as an obvious message to you that she needs to talk. Another idea may be a code word or phrase she can use in front of others. Clarify that this doesn't mean you will drop everything at that very moment to give her your full attention, but that it will mean that you will make time for her that night.

Sometimes this may mean that you have to stay up past pumpkin time to finish the presentation for tomorrow's meeting or fold the last load of laundry. Consider it an investment in your daughter's confidence that she can come to you with anything. Remember those nights when she would cry to be fed at 3:00 am even though you just fed her at 2:15 am? You ran to her side then, and she will appreciate knowing that you will do the same for her now.

#3 Show her that you respect her privacy, within reason.

Privacy in the teenage world is a privilege and not a right. Ask often for the Holy Spirit's guidance on when to assert some investigatory skills and when to back off. St. Don Bosco is one of my favorite role models for parenting. While he was neither married, nor had any children he ran an "oratory" where he housed hundreds of boys in Turin, Italy. Don Bosco's oratory was known for its infectious joy born in holiness. The boys who lived there thrived on happiness and sanctity. This is exactly the environment I hope to find in my own home! Don Bosco had two areas where he had no tolerance. The first of these was bad friends. Don Bosco knew that he couldn't compete with the peers that the boys chose to surround themselves with. He believed St. Paul when he said in 1 Cor. 15:33, "Do not be deceived: 'Bad company ruins good morals.'"

Secondly, Don Bosco did not allow any bad media within his establishment. He knew that we "consume" media and that we therefore, "are what we eat." This was the 1800s, and surely the threats to his boys came in the form of books. Our teens are exposing themselves to an avalanche of media each and every day. A grand percentage of which is not helping them grow in holiness. Your role as a parent is to discern who has access to what and when within your household. I heard the preacher Tony Evans once describe media with the following analogy. Imagine that you decide to stop cleaning your house entirely. You never even wash a dish or take out the trash. It won't be long before the roaches and the rats find pleasure indulging themselves in your household. If you invite garbage in the form of the media in your home you cannot be surprised when the devil shows up.

Cleary these two areas provide quite a challenge in the parenting and privacy department! Remember though, our teens in this age are making mostly everything about their lives public via social media. If their online "friends" or "followers" have access to their information, so should you. Don't be afraid to occasionally win the "Meanest Mom on the Block Award." The fight you may meet with your daughter has a reward if you are the winner, and it consists of a heart that is guarded by its mother.

However, the best way to be successful in this matter is by showing your daughter that you respect her privacy where it is due. A healthy balance is important in any relationship. For example, Journals and diaries are generally off-limits except in extreme situations where one might feel their child is an imminent danger to themselves. Additionally, don't ask to read her letters to her Husband-To-Be. If she offers, consider that a huge blessing and accept and follow-up with a load of affirmation.

#4 If possible, involve her Dad

It is often said that girls will, "marry their father." For some this is comforting, for others disheartening. Wherever your daughter's relationship is with her father, God can use it to convict her in her search for her Husband To Be. Fathers can teach us exactly what we want or define what we don't want in our future spouse. If your daughter's father is present in her life, be sure he is aware of the opportunity at hand. You are breaking open this topic with your daughter therefore opening a door for him. Invite him to initiate a conversation with her to be sure she knows he values her purity.

By the end of this booklet you will have many memories of conversations and prayers with your daughter. Invite her father to take the lead in the climactic moment at the conclusion of this booklet. The twelfth conversation in this book should be a definitive moment in your daughter's life. As mother and father you will ask your daughter to let you walk this journey to her vocation with her. You will ask for permission to guard her heart and share in the joy of God's plan for her.

She will then receive a ring as a placeholder for the one that will come in the future.

If her father is not present in her life be sure to address this when the topic arises. Ask her how she feels this will affect her future relationships and give her a chance to express her fears. God in is goodness is a Father. Whether your daughter's father is alive, deceased, active, unengaged, affectionate or distant the Lord can and will render amazing fruits for your daughter's future if she allows Him to. My story is an illustration of that. God is a Father who keeps His promises when we give Him the chance.

#5 Look for teaching moments **every single day**

Don't limit these conversations to official meetings behind closed doors. The more you talk to each other the more natural it will become. There will be no shortage of moments for you to discuss sexuality with your daughter. Whether it is the story about the girl who wore such short shorts to school, the billboard for the tanning salon or the gutter-mouthed DJ on the radio, you will have more opportunities than you can ever image if you start to look for them.

For example, if you choose to let your child watch a racier show, ignore the dishes and plop yourself on the couch to watch it with her. Get your money's worth on the DVR's "Pause" button and never miss an opportunity to discuss. Most importantly, **give your children the tools** to learn how to filter themselves. More than likely, your teen has been desensitized to the inundation of inappropriate content in the TV, movies, peer conversations, internet and music they consume. Help them recognize its prevalence and challenge them to react rather than that messages at face value.

#6 "Discuss" has two sides

Some moms just love to talk. Turn up the nervousness and they might never stop. Be careful to avoid turning this opportunity into "Twelve Preaching Sessions Every Mother Should Have With Their Daughter".

Listen to your daughter's opinions. Ask open ended questions. While she answers your questions search for follow-up questions.

Try:

- ❖ "Tell me more about that."
- ❖ "Why do you feel that way?"
- ❖ "Can you give me an example?"
- ❖ "What do you think is the root of that?"

If she doesn't agree with a particular point resist the temptation to quickly correct her and instead ask her to elaborate. In the best case scenario you can see if you can ask the right questions to help her arrive at the moral conclusion herself. If not, see if you can at least come to understand one another even if it doesn't mean you agree. Showing her that you respect her will go a **long** way in your ability to converse in the future.

#7 Define your approach and be sure all of your reactions align with that mission.

Ask yourself- what do you hope to accomplish during a discussion with your daughter about sexuality? Only you can answer this question. Whatever your answer is, make it your battle cry. Keep it right in the very front of your mind no matter what direction the conversation turns.

If you get uncomfortable, remember your mission. If you become defensive, remember your mission. If you become unsure of yourself, remember your mission. If your daughter asks a tough question, remember your mission. Be sure everything you say agrees with this mission and nothing gets in the way of it.

Examples may include:

I am doing this so that:

- ❖ My daughter can enjoy the eternal glory of Heaven.

- ❖ My daughter can protect her health and body.
- ❖ I can teach her to guard her heart.
- ❖ We can grow in our relationship with one another and she can know I am here for her in any circumstance.

Some key suggestions to consider as you define your mission:

- ❖ You held your daughter's hands as she toddled along learning how to take her first steps. You couldn't go ahead of her but instead you had to walk with her. Be sure she knows you are by her side no matter what.
- ❖ God has an incredible plan for you. He has an incredible plan for your daughter. He wants to share in this journey with you
- ❖ God's mercy is beyond our understanding. Have you ever really stopped to think about what it means that Christ died on the Cross for **every** sin? Think of the worst sin imaginable… He died and rose for that sin as well. Your daughter will understand this mercy in a greater way if she experiences it. God has chosen you to be the vessel to teach her this in word and action.

Take a few moments to think and pray about your mission statement for this time with your child. Write it here:

_____

#8 Qualify yourself

This statement has an important dual meaning. If you want your daughter to believe what you have to say, you must exhibit it in yourself. You have to find the quality in the mirror if you want her to believe she has it too.

Take some time for a self-image check. Our teenage daughters are plagued by the watchful eyes of others. It seems that even as adult women we have a hard time shaking those memories. Kids trust their parents and follow their example. During the 2008 elections, a co-worker and I had some great conversations about the political musings of her second grader and her classmates. It became clear that these seven year olds were listening to more of their parent's discussions than they realized. If I tell my preschooler that it is going to snow marshmallows in the morning, she will run to the window upon awakening with great expectations. Our kids listen to us. They trust us. They believe us even when we don't know they are listening. If you exhibit poor self-image, your example will be loud and clear to your daughter.

Make a resolve to be careful about your comments about her skinny legs or widow's peak. However rise to the greater challenge; be careful about your comments about yourself. You get to teach your daughter how to handle stretch marks, crow's feet and those first silver sprouts. If you are critical of your own reflection you can expect her to be critical of hers. Your confidence in your positive qualities will qualify you as a source worth listening to.

How To Use The Mother's Companion

There are many ways to use this guide to break open *Woman in Love* with your daughter. Some of my personal suggestions are below.

Who:

Woman in Love was written for young women of all faith levels and ages. In particular, I hoped to meet the needs of girls in their teens and twenties as they pursue their discernment of vocation. Below is a further breakdown of these age groups to help you decide how to approach *Woman in Love*.

High School - Young Adult- It's best to start early, but it's never too late. Woman in Love was written with this age group in mind!

Sixth Grade- I would recommend that mothers of sixth graders read *Woman in Love* independently. You can then pick and choose the topics that you feel are important at this time of her life. For example, the topic of modesty will probably top your list while the issues of Sexually Transmitted Diseases may wait for a later date. Just remember, you want to stay ahead of your daughter and her peers in the purity battle. If she hasn't already been inundated by the culture she will sooner than you wish!

Seventh Grade- Mothers may choose to read ahead of their daughters. Your teen can read the book after you complete if you feel she is ready. Honestly, in my dealings with middle school students, I believe seventh grade is the ideal time to catch them with the beauty of purity.

Eighth Grade- As a friend once told me, "By eighth grade, the horse has left the barn." Unfortunately, eighth grade seems to be the time that puberty and hormones officially take over the common sense section of the middle school brain. This may or may not mean that your daughter has opportunities to make poor decisions regarding her purity, but it definitely means that her peers are most likely talking about it. Depending on your comfort level, read ahead of or with your daughter.

Is your daughter ready for *Woman in Love*?

Only you can answer this question! Here are a few questions to help you discern:

Does your daughter have older siblings, cousins, neighbors or friends who have older acquaintances?

Unfortunately, this may mean she could be exposed to knowledge earlier than you might imagine or want! Deciding to talk to your daughter about these tough topics will not only ensure that she hears it from you first, but will also encourage her to come to **you** when she has further questions or concerns. In this day and age we must be proactive, rather than reactive." This is hard. This is unfortunate. This challenges me as a fellow parent. However, as much as we wish we could control the influences of our children, we can only do so much. If you want to ensure that friends, siblings, cousins, television, internet, neighbors etc. aren't the first ones to inform your daughter about sexuality there is only one answer: to beat them to the punch.

How Woman in Love can help: The over-arching message of Woman in Love is an invitation to fall madly in love with Christ. In doing so, I hope your daughter to find Him as her first influence in decision making.

Tip for further action: Familiarize yourself with the people your child loves and let them know you care about them because your daughter does.

Does she have a cell phone?

When I was a teenager I coveted the few friends I knew who had their own landline. I have since asked myself, "Why"? A few reasons come to mind a) privacy b) freedom. Enough said.

I will never forget a day when a teen in my youth ministry program was standing frustrated in my office as he tried to get a hold of a friend who wasn't answering her phone. Dumbfounded, I asked, "Why don't you just call her house?" He looked at me as though I were from another planet and answered, "Are you kidding? What if her *mom* answers or something?" If your daughter has a cell phone, gone are the days of screening those calls... at least until after the bill comes.

How Woman in Love can help: *Woman in Love* aims to show young women how to be respected and how to conduct themselves as women in love with the Lord. The goal is to help them behave as ladies, even when no one is there to help them filter.

Tip for further action: My Father-In-Law is famous for saying, "Nothing good happens after midnight." This is probably true in the media world as well. Many families require their teens to leave their laptops and phones in the kitchen overnight to prevent temptation.

Does your daughter have online accounts that require passwords?

Q. What is the function of a password?
A. To keep others out.

If a site requires a password, this should raise your parental red flag. This means that your child will have the opportunity to privately share, receive and accidently or intentionally view information. This content may or may not be in line with the moral compass of your household.

How Woman in Love can help: The best thing you can do for your daughter is **communicate.** Yes, it would be easier to hide her in a cave. If you decide against this method, she will be exposed to the culture to some degree with or without the help of social networking. She needs your advice on how to filter the many messages of the world.

Tip for further action: If you choose to allow your child access to these sorts of sites and you feel they are age appropriate, you may be inclined to request that they share this password with you. This will help you guide them in the right direction. Another option is considering opening an account of your own so that you too can have the pleasure of "following" or "friending" your teenagers.

If your child is younger and you are inclined to allow them to participate consider a family account for e-mail, pinterest, instagram, facebook, tumblr, twitter, snapchat etc.

Does your daughter go to dances?

The latest craze in middle and high school dances is called "grinding". (Yes that **does** say middle school.) Grinding is defined by a "rubbing together of genital areas". The purpose of this "dance" is to simulate "dry" sex. The Washington Post explains:

"For those of you fortunate enough not to have had experience with this yet, here's what kids do today at many school dances (as well as at parties, formal and otherwise): They provocatively grind their pelvises into each other on the dance floor, sometimes standing face to face, sometimes with the boy behind the girl. It's called grinding.
But sometimes there is something more troubling going on: Boys often walk up to girls who don't already have a boy thrusting his genitals at them and just start right up, no permission sought. Many girls, who even in the 21st century will do nearly anything to win a boy's attention, allow them to go ahead without a word. Of course, there are some girls who initiate it themselves. That's no better"[i]

Grinding is prevalent in private and public school dances alike. Grinding is more of a rule than an exception. The teens talk about it leading up to the dance. They form circles around grinding couples to protect the prying eyes of teachers and chaperones. Teens feel stress about grinding or feeling ostracized if they refuse.

How Woman in Love can help: If your daughter is potentially exposed to grinding at dances or otherwise, it is probably time for deeper discussion about purity.

Tip for further action: Find out what your child's school policy is on preventing grinding. Most schools have some sort of action plan, but many aren't strictly enforced.

Does your daughter watch TV?

The average Teen will see 14,000 televised sexual references per year[ii] A 2001 report found that teens rank the media second only to school sex education programs as a leading source of information about sex.[iii] A 2004 report found that "the media far outranked parents or schools as the source of information about birth control.[iv] In television programming aimed at teens, more than 90% of episodes had at least one sexual reference with an average of 7.9 references per hour.[v] If your daughter watches movies, television or listens to mainstream radio your guidance on her absorption of these things is very much needed!

How Woman in Love can help: The media is often called the "Super Peer" as it is more effective than any other outside source to make it look like "everyone is doing it." *Woman in Love* aims to give young women a gauge regarding real expectations for love and marriage.

Tip for further action: Don't be afraid to say no to television and other media. Find creative ways to monitor the time spent. This may mean some sacrifices on your part as well! Giving up cable for Lent never killed anyone that I know of. A similar example that I have seen is changing the wifi password every day and only revealing it once certain chores are completed. Most importantly know what your kids are consuming and what it is teaching them.

But wait! I am still not sure I want my daughter thinking about her future *husband*! She is just so young to be thinking about such things!

"These commandments that I give you today are to be upon your hearts. Impress them on your children. Talk about them when you sit at home and when you walk along the road, when you lie down and when you get up." Deut. 6:6-7

Of course, this decision is completely yours. Not every middle or high school student may be ready for the message of *Woman in Love*. Prayerfully and **courageously** discern the level of discussion you believe your daughter is ready for. Below you will find several different methods and approaches to reading this book with your daughter. The chapter by chapter sessions can easily be adapted to fit your specific needs. As the wise saying goes, "Mother Knows Best."

Woman in Love is not meant to tempt young women to envision every crush at the foot of the alter on their wedding day. On the contrary, it encourages them to guard their heart until the due time. As her mother, you too want to guard this heart that first beat within your very body. The Lord chose your womb as the place to knit her heart together, and of course you want to be a part of the decision to give it away.

Our young women are under so much pressure. They want to be the best at their sport, make first chair in band, have a date to homecoming and have the best hair and body. Simultaneously, they are bombarded with challenges to do well in school, go to a great college and find a career. In the midst of all of the encouragement we have to ask ourselves what the ultimate goal is. If you asked most girls what they want out of life, they would answer, "I want to get married and have a family." Your daughter will only find one place where she will be molded, trained and encouraged in this life dream- under your roof. If you don't prepare her, it is likely that no one will. If the ultimate goal is to be a wife and mother, then it should require the ultimate preparation. This is where you come in.

The final chapter of *Woman in Love* is titled, "Your Reason." The entire conclusion of this book restates what has already been emphasized so vividly in the previous pages. It reminds young women to "keep their eye on the ball." Our daughters should have their eyes focused on **Christ** as their First Love, so that if they are called to marriage, He may lead them to their second.

Until recent history, dating had one purpose: courtship. Courtship generally began with an invitation to a young potential suitor to meet in the parlor of a young woman. The first meeting generally consisted of mother, daughter and gentleman in question. As time went on a companionship that was approved by parents would develop with the potential of marriage. Similarly, many parents prepared dowries for their daughter at her birth or practiced the tradition of a "hope chest". The hope chest was usually a trunk that a mother would begin to fill commencing when her daughter reached puberty. The hope chest and its contents would be given to her and her spouse upon their marriage. This may include linens, china, silver and even appropriate undergarments for married life.

It is evident that dating and marriage has been a family affair for ages. It wasn't until the last hundred years that "dating" began to move from the private setting of the home to the public setting of the world. While we can't change the cultural norms surrounding us, we can surely do our best to operate within them with our moral compass as our guide. It is my hope that this process will help you build a spiritual and emotional hope chest together with your daughter. I pray that you will begin to mold her dowry by giving her the tools to define dating and relationships by the standards you share with the Lord.

How:

The Chapter by Chapter Session Guide will provide you with chances to dive in to conversation with your daughter. The Mother's Companion does not seek to restate or elaborate on the material in *Woman in Love*. The goal of this booklet is to give you time to discuss *Woman In Love* as you read while simultaneously providing you with some opportunities to talk, pray, listen and learn about one another.

Each Session has three parts.

A. Before Meeting With Your Daughter
   ❖ *Prepare*- This section provides you with some thoughts to think and pray about prior to your time with your daughter.
B. With Your Daughter
   ❖ *Invite*- During your time with your daughter you will want to invite the presence of the Lord to guide and inspire you! This section will serve as the "opening prayer" portion of your time together
   ❖ *Discuss*- You will choose one of three ways to approach *Woman in Love* together (see below). During this section of your session you will talk about the points that stood out in your reading. Additionally, I have provided some other

talking points for each of you to consider in order to keep the discussion moving along.

❖ *Pray-* It may be cliché, but it is true what they say, "A family that prays together, stays together." The surest way to a close and confident relationship with your daughter is prayer. Whether this is something that is already a part of your relationship, or something you've never done before, this section will guide you!

C. After Meeting With Your Daughter

❖ *Take Action-* Put your heart on paper and journal about the ways you will pray for your daughter regarding each conversation you have.

There are four ways to break *Woman in Love* open together:

Option 1. For the younger reader: Mothers, go ahead and read *Woman in Love* ahead of your daughter. It is then that you can pick and choose the topics you feel your daughter is ready for. You will find that most of the Chapter by Chapter Session Guides are focused on giving you an opportunity to dive deeper in your relationship and communication with your daughter. They are easily adaptable to fit your comfort zone and your daughter's age. She will surely appreciate the opportunity to have alone time with you to talk about your relationship and her relationship with those around her. The rest of the content can be stashed away for later years.

Option 2. Read *Woman in Love* out loud together. Take time to answer questions that may come up or unpack concepts.

Option 3. Read one chapter at a time independently and come together to discuss. Each reader can highlight their copy (or highlight with a different color in the same copy) and then begin the discussion time by sharing what parts stood out and why.

Option 4. As I said earlier, Mother/Daughter relationships are complex and diverse. Each personality is different and often times mothers and teenage daughters tend to clash in their communication.

Trust me, this is typical and it doesn't mean you are doing a poor job in your role as mother. You may feel that your attempt to present this book and guide would do more harm than good. It is normal for some teens to be turned off to every suggestion their parents have for them. Should you feel this is the case for you, don't be discouraged. Give your daughter a copy of *Woman in Love* and read this Mother's Companion! Pray that the Holy Spirit will provide opportunities for you to bring the topics discussed in the following pages to her attention. This may mean casually mentioning something when you drive her to school, while you are cleaning up from dinner together or when you pick her up from soccer. **Most importantly, still make a point to execute the climax of this booklet found in the session for Chapter 12.** This will be a memorable event regardless of the conversation leading up to that point and could potentially change her life forever!

When:

Ah, perhaps the toughest question within these pages! Will all of this take some time? Most definitely. As Steve Bollman, founder of the Men's Program, That Man Is You! says, "How you spend your time is how you spend yourself." If you spend a dollar you can make another, but you can never get back your time. It is truly a gift of self. Reading ahead and preparing yourself for your discussions with your daughter will take time. Meeting with her will take time. Praying with and for her will take time. You will be investing, and you have to ask yourself if your goal is worth the price.

If the answer is yes, then pick a consistent schedule that will allow you and your daughter to make time to be together and talk about these important topics. The guide will offer you twelve sessions to align with the twelve chapters of the book. This doesn't have to be consecutive days although that may work best for you. Perhaps weekly or bi-weekly is more suitable. For example, you may choose, Wednesdays at 8:30 pm or Sunday mornings for a breakfast date.

Recognize that life is busy and demanding. Like all good things, this may take some sacrifice from both parties to make it work. We "make time" for a lot of things in our life: Social Media, our favorite shows, visiting with friends. Finding the time for both of you may mean scratching a thing or two for each party. Whatever you choose as your standard time, recognize that things may come up once or twice. Pick a backup plan ahead of time, in case there is too much homework or traffic. If a particular Wednesday doesn't work out, insist that you both assure one another that you will meet on Thursday.

Remember, God will never be outdone in generosity and your return on this investment begins now...

Conversation One

My First Love

❖ Hebrews 11:1 Faith is being sure of what we hope for and certain of what we do not see.

❖ Romans 8:28 All things work together for good for those who love the Lord.

❖ Matthew 7:9-11 Which one of you would hand his son a stone when he asks for a loaf of bread, or a snake when he asks for a fish? If you then, who are wicked, know how to give good gifts to your children, how much more will your heavenly Father give good things to those who ask Him.

❖ Matthew 6:26 Look at the birds in the sky; they do not sow or reap, they gather nothing into barns, yet your heavenly Father feeds them. Are not you more important than they?

Before meeting with your daughter:

Conversation One- Goal: To break the ice and set the tone for discussion, openness and prayer.

Prepare:

Self-denial. This is the word that sums up every meal gone cold while you attend to your family's needs, the bloodshot eyes from nighttime feedings, the clean-ups from the stomach flu, and the late night help with projects that should have been started weeks ago. It is the word that best describes "motherhood". As a good priest friend of mine once said, "we give and we give and we give, and then we die."

Why? Because we love.

It is natural to let go of ourselves, and unnatural to let go of our children. We deny ourselves so we can give them the best. We have plans for them, and hopes for their future! In some ways we know them better than they know themselves.

God is a Father, and He designed parenthood to teach us about Himself. He too gave everything for your children. Indeed, He gave **His** own Child as ransom for **your** daughter. He loves even more than you do, has sacrificed even more than you have, and has even more hope and plans for what is ahead. He wants to lay His desires for your daughter on your heart. He wants to breathe His Spirit in you continually and unite your sacrifices to His cross. Read Jeremiah 29:11. Pray for the courage and desire to release your plans for your daughter to the Lord. Ask for the strength to marry your will to His in every way. Know that you can trust Him!

Notes:

Reflect on the "selfless love" you feel for this particular child. What about her makes these sacrifices worth it? Additionally, use these "notes" sections to write any thoughts on the chapter or ideas regarding the "discuss" section on the following page.

_____

_____

_____

_____

_____

_____

_____

_____

_____

With Your Daughter:

Invite:

Remember Jesus' promise, "For where two or three are gathered in my name, there am I among them," Matthew 18:20. Pray out loud inviting the Lord to be with you during this time together:

Lord, you have chosen a specific vocation for each of us and given us specific gifts that will aid us in your call. You know where we will find the most joy and fulfillment in this life you freely gave to us. Moreover, we did not choose each other, you have chosen us, mother and daughter, for one another. Although we may not always see eye to eye, we are thankful for the gift of our relationship. We invite you into our home, into this room, into this discussion, into our hearts and into our relationship. We ask that you will show us your path and help us to always guide each other on our journey to holiness. We love you Jesus and we wish to love you more. Amen.

Discuss:

- ❖ Begin with a general sharing on Chapter One according to the method you have chosen to follow.
    - o Take your time and write notes in the margin as you go! These memories will be a treasure for you one day!
    - o Don't be afraid to develop any topic that may arise. Sometimes the Holy Spirit works tangentially, starting us out in one spot and delivering us to a place He wants us to go!
- ❖ Read Jeremiah 29:11
    - o Ask your daughter if she asks God's opinion when she has a decision to make. Why or why not?

o How can each of you give flesh to Jeremiah 29:11 today? What weighs on your heart that you can entrust to Him?

Pray:

❖ Take turns praying out loud. Moms- take the lead and set an example. Explain to your daughter that prayer doesn't have to be eloquent, it just has to be honest. This may be uncomfortable at first, but this is because prayer is intimate. If you open yourself up spiritually, the fruits will follow.

❖ As you pray ask the Lord for His Will in your daughter's life. Ask most especially for the courage to trust in it.

❖ Offer any special intentions either of you may have.

After meeting with your daughter

What I learned about my daughter today:

_____

_____

_____

_____

_____

How I am going to pray for my daughter based on this conversation:

_____

_____

_____

_____

_____

_____

Conversation Two

God's Faithfulness In Suffering

Peer Pressure:
Ps 60:12
Ps 56:3-4
1 Pet 4:14
Ps 84:11

Self Image:
1 John 3:1
Eph. 2:10
Ps 139:14

Stress:
Is 40:29-31
Rom 15:13
Ps 29:11
Ps 27:5
Mt 11:28
Prv 12:25

Before meeting with your daughter:

Conversation Two- Goal: To establish or deepen trust through discussing one another's relationship with God.

Prepare:

The "Dear HTB" section of this chapter invites your daughter to share her faith story. What is your testimony? Who were you before you encountered Christ? What happened to change you? How have things been different since? Take some time to pray through your testimony before you sit with your daughter. Quietly listen for the Lord to bring back good and bad memories. Let Him grant 20/20 vision to your hindsight as He discloses the ways He was present even when you didn't recognize it at the time. Write out your testimony and use it to open up to your daughter today.

Testimonies shouldn't be too long, maybe five to ten minutes. A good testimony generally has three parts. About 25% should describe life before Christ. Generalizations are fine and details aren't needed. Half of the story should center on what happened to change your heart and the last quarter focuses on how your life has been impacted by His presence. She may have never heard this story before, or she may have heard it a million times. Regardless, this is a chance to openly tell your daughter what joy you hope the Lord will bestow in her life as well.

Notes:

Write your testimony here. You may also want to read the *Discuss* section below and jot down any notes you may want to address from Chapter Two.

_____

_____

_____

_____

_____

_____

_____

_____

_____

_____

_____

_____

With Your Daughter:

Invite:

Open in prayer. Call upon the Holy Spirit to be in your presence.

"Come Holy Spirit, fill the hearts of your faithful and kindle in them the fire of your love. Send forth your Spirit and they shall be created. And You shall renew the face of the earth. Amen"

Discuss:

❖ Begin by breaking open your copy of *Woman in Love*. Discuss the content of Chapter 2 that stood out to the two of you.

❖ Share your testimony with your daughter. Ask her to share hers with you. If she has trouble articulating her story, discuss the questions in paragraph three on page 27 of *Woman in Love*.

❖ Inquire about your daughter's relationship with God. Ask her to describe it.

　　o What is her favorite name for God? Is she close enough to give Him a name? Is He more of a Master or a Merciful Father?

❖ Ask your daughter what she is struggling with.

❖ Her answer may surprise you. She may be struggling with friendships or self-image. On the other hand she may be nervous about managing her time at her locker or that it's a volleyball unit in P.E. and she just hates volleyball.

❖ Remember, you have the perspective and life experience to know that some of your daughter's worries are not a big deal- <u>she doesn't</u>. They **are** a big deal to her. One of the biggest complaints from teens is that their parent's "don't understand". Validate her feelings even when you know it's small stuff in the long run. As the popular quote says, "If you let your kids tell you the small stuff now, they will want to tell you the big stuff when they get older. To them, it has always been big stuff."

Pray:

- ❖ Ask your daughter if she is willing to trust that God is walking with her.
- ❖ Take turns praying out loud with your daughter. If she answered yes to the question above ask the Lord to reveal the ways He is with her. If she answered no, that is ok too. Ask for a greater desire for trust.
- ❖ Offer any specific intentions or decisions that are weighing on each of your hearts.

After meeting with your daughter

What I learned about my daughter today:

_____

_____

_____

_____

_____

How I am going to pray for my daughter based on this conversation:

_____

_____

_____

_____

_____

_____

Conversation Three

On My Own
& All Alone

❖ Titus 2:4-5 Similarly, older women should be reverent in their behavior, not slanderers, not addicted to drink, teaching what is good, so that they may train younger women to love their husbands and children, to be self-controlled, chaste, good homemakers, under the control of their husbands, so that the word of God may not be discredited

❖ Matthew 10:16 Behold, I am sending you like sheep in the midst of wolves; so be shrewd as serpents and simple as doves.

❖ Ruth 1:16 Wherever you go I will go, wherever you stay I will stay. Your people shall be my people and your God, my God. (Spoken by the widow Ruth to her Mother-in-law and caretaker.)

❖ Ephesians 6:1 Children, obey your parents

❖ Mt 18:6 Whoever causes one of these little ones who believe in me to sin, it would be better for him to have a great millstone hung around his neck and to be drowned in the depths of the sea.

Before meeting with your daughter:

Conversation Three- Goal: To establish a clear
understanding of your guidelines for dating and relationships.

Prepare:

Ask yourself, what are your dating guidelines as a parent? Are they developed? Do you and your daughter's father agree? Is your daughter aware of these guidelines? Examples of this may include:

- ❖ Age when dating is allowed
- ❖ Appropriate locations for dates
- ❖ Whether or not you allow individual dates or only group dates
- ❖ Appropriate clothing for dates
- ❖ If she is allowed to initiate calls or speak to boys on the phone
- ❖ Times she can communicate with boys on the phone or in person
- ❖ Whether or not you have to meet a boy before they can date

Setting up specific rules for your daughter will help develop an understanding that she must set up boundaries for herself when you aren't around to help her make tough decisions. St. John Bosco is known for his "oratory" in Italy where he housed and catechized hundreds of young boys. The oratory was well known for its contagious joy and infectious holiness. Father Bosco had a motto for his boys, "Make it easy for them to be good and hard for them to be bad." This should be our motto for parenting. If we provide opportunities for good choices and lessen opportunities for poor ones, we give our children an environment conducive to success.

A suggestion that I just love involves allowing your daughter to invite her interest over as a friend to spend time with the family. Welcome him to join you for Mass and lunch on Sunday. If he is willing to do this, it shows that he is respectful of your family, your rules and your daughter. If he doesn't feel comfortable or is embarrassed to do so it is probably a red flag. If he doesn't respect these guidelines then you shouldn't anticipate that he will respect your daughter.

Prepare for pushback. Decide ahead of time where you and her father are willing to dialogue or ask her what she believes to be reasonable. How will you answer when she questions your trust in her? Be sure you stick to that mission statement. What is the goal of all of this?

Notes:

Write your take on reasonable dating guidelines in your family:

_____

_____

_____

_____

_____

_____

_____

_____

_____

_____

_____

With Your Daughter:

Invite:

Mary is the perfect mother and the perfect woman. It is so appropriate to look to her for guidance and ask her to pray for us within this journey. Our Catholic tradition provides us with ten virtues of Mary to meditate on and attempt to possess ourselves. For the next ten sessions we will choose one of those virtues to contemplate and strive for in our own lives.

Virtue of Mary: Ardent Charity: Letting her love for God be the driving force behind every decision

Spend sixty seconds in silence thinking about what Ardent Charity means in your life and inviting Mary to teach you.

"Come, Holy Spirit. Bring the gift of Ardent Charity. Guide our conversation tonight. Blessed Mother, pray for us that we may please God by becoming more like you.

Hail Mary, full of grace the Lord is with you. Blessed are you among women and blessed is the fruit of your womb, Jesus. Holy Mary, Mother of God, pray for us sinners, now and at the hour of our death. Amen"

Discuss:

❖ Begin by breaking open Chapter 3 together. Discuss the parts that stood out to both of you and develop the themes that come up in conversation.

❖ Discuss your dating guidelines with your daughter. If she is not of dating age, let her know some of the guidelines that will affect her first when she begins to date. This way she isn't caught off guard by your reaction if her crush "asks her out."

❖ Talk about what purpose "dating" has in middle school? How about High School? College?

❖ How does dating at each of these stages prepare you for your vocation?

❖ How does dating at each of these stages bring you closer to God?

❖ How can breaking up with someone affect you in a positive or negative way?

❖ What do you think God intends for dating relationships at each of these stages?

Pray:

One of my favorite Saints is Saint Philomena. Philomena was a princess in ancient Greece during the reign of the tyrant, Diocletian. For fear of Diocletian's army, Philomena's parents offered her to the Roman Emperor to be his bride. The young princess held fast to her commitment to be a bride of Christ and remain a virgin married to the Lord. For her defiance the Emperor had her imprisoned, scourged like the spouse she preferred to him, thrown into the river and shot with arrows. During each attempt on her life, and the physical pain and suffering that accompanied it, the Lord delivered her. She was eventually martyred by beheading and her soul was thrust into the arms of the Lord. Saint Philomena has is known for her, "Courageous Purity" and "Steadfast Faith." What more can we ask for our daughters?!

On the day Mark and I were married my mother-in-law hugged me, looked me in the eye and said, "Girl, I have been praying for you since before you were born." The Lord hears the relentless prayers of a mother! Today will begin a novena asking for Saint Philomena to intercede for your daughter and her future husband. A novena is nine days of prayers uttered for a single intention. Pray the following prayers out loud together.

Novena for the Intercession of Saint Philomena (Based on the prayer composed by Saint John Vianney)

Saint Philomena! Your life and death gave great glory to the Lord. I rejoice in the ways He has used your witness to inspire generations in their vow of purity. Through this novena I pray that I may come to know you as my sister, my guide, my companion and ally. As I come to you for aid today, I realize that it is not me who discovered you, but you who desire to pray for me. I want to commit myself to purity, but I cannot do it alone. You chose to give your very life for the sake of chastity. Be by my side as I face temptations, pressures and perhaps even ridicule for this decision I have made.

Pray for me particularly, that I may exhibit an unbreakable purity, and strength of soul that is always invincible in every kind of assault. Pray that I may have the generosity to give the Lord every sacrifice. Pray that I will have a love as strong as death for Jesus Christ.

Please pray beside me for these intentions and in addition, if I am called to marriage, I ask for your prayers for my future spouse. Bring these same requests to the heart of our Lord whom you love so much.

God is so good that you gave your blood and your life for Him. God has been so good and so generous to you, and we pray that He will also be so generous to us! He has loved me so much it cost Him His life. He has loved me so much that He has given Himself to live in me in the Eucharist. He has loved me so much that He has given me every good and perfect gift in my life. Surely, He will never be deaf to your prayers, nor to mine. Full of confidence, I imitate you as I place all my trust in Him. Amen

FIRST DAY- Take a moment in silence to consider that Saint Philomena was a virgin: She was a virgin in such a world and in such an age. She was a virgin in spite of persecution and a virgin until death. Ask for the grace to endure whatever sacrifices may come your way.

Close by praying out loud for any intentions each of you may have.

After meeting with your daughter:

What I learned about my daughter today:

_____

_____

_____

How I am going to pray for my daughter based on this particular conversation:

_____

_____

_____

_____

Prayers I have seen answered since we've begun this journey:

_____

_____

_____

Conversation Four

Wounded and In Love

- ❖ Ephesians 2:10 We are God's workmanship created in Christ Jesus to do good works which God prepared us in advance to do.
- ❖ Jer 1: 7-9 But the LORD answered me, Do not say, "I am too young." To whomever I send you, you shall go; whatever I command you, you shall speak. Do not be afraid of them, for I am with you to deliver you—oracle of the LORD. Then the LORD extended his hand and touched my mouth, saying to me, See, I place my words in your mouth!
- ❖ Is 54:5 For your husband is your Maker; the LORD of hosts is his name, Your redeemer, the Holy One of Israel, called God of all the earth.
- ❖ 1 Cor 7:32 I should like you to be free of anxieties. An unmarried man is anxious about the things of the Lord, how he may please the Lord.
- ❖ "If you are what you should be, you will set the whole world on fire!" -St. Catherine of Sienna

Before meeting with your daughter:

Conversation Four- Goal: To teach your daughter how to possess a spirit of discernment for God's Will in her life.

Prepare:

I have heard many parents distress over their personal fear that their children may be called to religious life. How do you feel about this particular topic? If you find yourself less than excited try to identify the source of your trepidation.

Blessed Louis Martin is the father of the beloved Saint Therese. Louis and his wife, Blessed Zelie Martin, had five daughters, four of whom became Carmelite nuns and the other joined the order of the Poor Clares. In humility he asked, "Who am I that the Lord should chose His brides from among my daughters?" What an honor; what a blessing!

Lead by example; show your daughter in your prayer that you want to say "Yes!" to His Will in your own life! When you close in prayer tonight be vulnerable. Pray for something personal. For example, you may ask for help with patience dealing with a co-worker, for God's Will concerning a stress about her dad's job, or even something that may sound trivial but is causing you anxiety. Show her that you want God to lead you as well.

Notes:

Write down some discussion notes for yourself. Reflect on the discussion points in the following pages. In particular, ask if you willing to say "yes" to God's call for your daughter no matter what it is? If not what can you work on to get you to this point?

_____

_____

_____

_____

_____

_____

_____

_____

_____

With your daughter:

Invite:

Virtue of Mary: Blind Obedience: Following God's call without counting the cost

Spend sixty seconds in silence thinking about what Blind Obedience means in your life and invite Mary to teach you.

"Come, Holy Spirit. Bring the gift of Blind Obedience. Guide our conversation tonight. Blessed Mother, pray for us that we may please God by becoming more like you.

Hail Mary, full of grace the Lord is with you. Blessed are you among women and blessed is the fruit of your womb, Jesus. Holy Mary, Mother of God, pray for us sinners, now and at the hour of our death. Amen"

Discuss:

❖ Talk through your thoughts on Chapter Four. Discuss any topics that may come up. Reminder- don't be afraid of productive tangents centered on good topics. Don't limit the Holy Spirit in the subject matter He may want to bring up.
❖ Share your thoughts on vocation to Religious Life and ask your daughter to share hers.

❖ Remember- Jesus is our first love and doesn't disappoint. Ask your daughter if she trusts that, regardless of what her vocation is, that He is the man strong enough to handle all her fears, joys, pains and triumphs.

❖ Ask your daughter what her greatest stumbling block would be if the Lord called her to Religious Life.

❖ Remind her that nuns and priests don't wake up each day thinking, "Man, I am sad I am not married with a family." God fills them and gives them joy, not regret!

❖ Discuss-are you willing to trust in the Lord and say "Yes" whatever His call? If not, what can you work on to get you to that point?

Pray:

When I was in high school I stressed a great deal about discovering my vocational call. One night in prayer I realized that if the Lord told me my calling at that moment I would have no ability to act on it at all. Instead I would just be anxious about the future either way. I resolved instead to spend my time preparing myself for the moment He would call.

Pray for clarity to do God's Will when He calls. Most importantly however, ask for the courage to do God's Will at every moment of your life. Condition yourself to always listen for His voice and be ready to answer.

Novena for the Intercession of Saint Philomena

Saint Philomena! Your life and death gave great glory to the Lord. I rejoice in the ways He has used your witness to inspire generations in their vow of purity. Through this novena I pray that I may come to know you as my sister, my guide, my companion and ally. As I come to you for aid today, I realize that it is not me who discovered you, but you who desire to pray for me. I want to commit myself to purity, but I cannot do it alone. You chose to give your very life for the sake of chastity. Be by my side as I face temptations, pressures and perhaps even ridicule for this decision I have made.

Pray for me particularly, that I may exhibit an unbreakable purity, and strength of soul that is always invincible in every kind of assault. Pray that I may have a generosity to give the Lord every sacrifice. Pray that I will have a love as strong as death for Jesus Christ.

Please pray beside me for these intentions and in addition, if I am called to marriage, I ask for your prayers for my future spouse. Bring these same requests to the heart of our Lord whom you love so much.

God is so good that you gave your blood and your life for Him. God has been so good and so generous to you, and we pray that He will also be so generous to us! He has loved me so much it cost Him His life. He has loved me so much that He has given Himself to live in me in the Eucharist. He loved me so much that He has given me every good and perfect gift in my life. Surely, He will never be deaf to your prayers, nor to mine. Full of confidence, I imitate you as I place all my trust in Him. Amen

SECOND DAY

Take a few minutes to silently consider that Saint Philomena was strong in her resolve to be chaste. She knew how to control her desires. Philomena knew she must avoid the near occasion of sin. What are the sources of your temptations, weaknesses, anxieties and falls? They may be media, outfit choices, friends, boundaries with the opposite sex etc. Ask how the Lord wants you to eliminate these sources?

Close by praying out loud for any intentions each of you may have.

After meeting with your daughter:

What I learned about my daughter today:

_____

_____

_____

How I am going to pray for my daughter based on this particular conversation:

_____

_____

_____

_____

Prayers I have seen answered since we've begun this journey:

_____

_____

_____

Conversation Five

All Things New

❖ Prv 31: 10, 11a, 12, 20, 25, 26, 28, 30 Who can find a woman of
worth? Far beyond jewels is her value. Her husband trusts her
judgment... She brings him profit, not loss, all the days of her life.
She reaches out her hands to the poor, and extends her arms to the
needy. She is clothed with strength and dignity, and laughs at the
days to come. She opens her mouth in wisdom; kindly instruction is
on her tongue. Her children rise up and call her blessed; her
husband, too, praises her. Charm is deceptive and beauty fleeting;
the woman who fears the LORD is to be praised.

❖ Lk 2:5 His mother said to the servers, "Do whatever he tells you."
(Mary's last words in scripture.)

Before meeting with your daughter:

Conversation Five- Goal: To set a clear image of the woman your daughter wants to be.

Prepare:

If you want your daughter to be pure, the Blessed Mother is your ticket. The flesh that was nailed to the cross for our salvation was made in Mary's womb. Your daughter's body was formed in yours. You now want her to protect it. In today's session we will ask the Blessed Mother to be a role model for both you, and your daughter..

It isn't every day that you get to gush about your daughter. Write down some qualities that you cherish and admire about her. Prepare to express your love as mother. As the popular quote says, "You will never know the depth of my love for you. You are the only one who knows the sound of my heart from the inside."

Notes:

List some affirmations for your daughter. Pray particularly on the third discussion point in the *Discuss* section below. Jot down your thoughts in the space below.

_____

_____

_____

_____

_____

_____

_____

_____

_____

_____

_____

_____

_____

_____

With your daughter:

Invite:

Virtue of Mary: Profound Humility: Knowing who she is before God, nothing more and nothing less

Spend sixty seconds in silence thinking about what Profound Humility means in your life and invite Mary to teach you.

"Come, Holy Spirit. Bring the gift of Profound Humility. Guide our conversation tonight. Blessed Mother, pray for us that we may please God by becoming more like you.

Hail Mary, full of grace the Lord is with you. Blessed are you among women and blessed is the fruit of your womb, Jesus. Holy Mary, Mother of God, pray for us sinners, now and at the hour of our death. Amen"

Discuss:
   ❖ Reflect on your thoughts on Chapter 5. Discuss any topics that may come up.

   ❖ Ask your daughter to name a woman she admires and ask her why.

   ❖ Invite her to list some qualities she hopes to have a grown woman.

   o   Ask- how will she ensure this will happen?

     o   Ask your daughter; What decisions need to be made to guarantee you turn into the woman you want to be?

❖ Talk to you daughter about the love of a Mother. Shower your daughter with affirmation and ask her to allow you to walk this journey with her.

❖ Mary was a mother too. She knows Christ better than anyone on earth! She wants to reveal Him to the two of you.

     o   Discuss how you can bring Mary into your home more concretely. Brainstorm with your daughter and make a decision together.

❖ An example may be printing and framing the Ten Virtues of Mary and displaying them in your bathroom so you can clothe yourself in them as you get ready in the morning. Maybe you purchase matching rosaries and keep them in your pockets so that you can reach in and "hold Mary's hand" during the day. Perhaps you will decide to pray a rosary novena together for the nine days leading up to the next Marian Feast Day.

❖ Write your commitment here:

Pray:

Novena for the Intercession of Saint Philomena

Saint Philomena! Your life and death gave great glory to the Lord. I rejoice in the ways He has used your witness to inspire generations in their vow of purity. Through this novena I pray that I may come to know you as my sister, my guide, my companion and ally. As I come to you for aid today, I realize that it is not me who discovered you, but you who desire to pray for me. I want to commit myself to purity, but I cannot do it alone. You chose to give your very life for the sake of chastity. Be by my side as I face temptations, pressures and perhaps even ridicule for this decision I have made.

Pray for me particularly, that I may exhibit an unbreakable purity, and strength of soul that is always invincible in every kind of assault. Pray that I may have a generosity to give the Lord every sacrifice. Pray that I will have a love as strong as death for Jesus Christ.

Please pray beside me for these intentions and in addition, if I am called to marriage, I ask for your prayers for my future spouse. Bring these same requests to the heart of our Lord whom you love so much.

God is so good that you gave your blood and your life for Him. God has been so good and so generous to you, and we pray that He will also be so generous to us! He has loved me so much it cost Him His life. He has loved me so much that He has given Himself to live in me in the Eucharist. He loved me so much that He has given me every good and perfect gift in my life. Surely, He will never be deaf to your prayers, nor to mine. Full of confidence, I imitate you as I place all my trust in Him. Amen

THIRD DAY

Silently consider that Saint Philomena preserved and increased the love which she had for chastity by means of prayer and the Sacraments. It is here that the soul is washed in the Blood of Jesus Christ, and is nourished with His Sacred Body. Through these reminders she never forgot that her body was the temple of the Holy Spirit. You too have these weapons at your disposal. How can you better use them to remind you that the Holy Spirit lives within you at all times?

Close by praying out loud for any intentions each of you may have.

After meeting with your daughter:

What I learned about my daughter today:

_____

_____

_____

How I am going to pray for my daughter based on this particular conversation:

_____

_____

_____

_____

Prayers I have seen answered since we've begun this journey:

_____

_____

_____

_____

Conversation Six

Woman in Love

- ❖ Tobit 8:5-8 "Blessed are you, O God of our ancestors; blessed be your name forever and ever! Let the heavens and all your creation bless you forever. You made Adam, and you made his wife Eve to be his helper and support; and from these two the human race has come. You said, 'It is not good for the man to be alone; let us make him a helper like himself.' Now, not with lust, but with fidelity I take this kinswoman as my wife. Send down your mercy on me and on her, and grant that we may grow old together. Bless us with children." They said together, "Amen, amen!" (Tobiah and his wife Sarah pray this prayer on their wedding night)
- ❖ Eph 5:25 Husbands, love your wives, even as Christ loved the church and handed himself over for her.
- ❖ Song of Songs 8:6 Set me as a seal upon your heart, as a seal upon your arm; For Love is strong as Death, unyielding as the grave. Its arrows are arrows of fire, flames of the divine. Deep waters cannot quench love, nor rivers sweep it away.

Before Meeting With Your Daughter:

Conversation Six- Goal: To show your daughter that you

want to be a part of her discernment of not only her vocation, but of the man she chooses if she is called to marriage.

Prepare:

During your preparations to discuss Chapter 5, you made a list of the things you love about your daughter. For this Chapter make a list of qualities that you hope for in her future spouse. Make sure you include the obvious ones: respectful, honest, God-fearing etc. Don't stop there. Challenge yourself to think of some attributes that will compliment the qualities that you listed about your daughter. If she is shy, talk about your desire for a man who will make her laugh and dance in the rain. Tell her that you want her to find a man who tells her she is beautiful every day. List some qualities that you hope he will have as a father. Be sure to include some fun ones too. You may think of ways he might dress or hobbies he may have. This will make for an even more entertaining discussion!

Notes:

Write your wish list for your future Son-in-law. Include a prayer that he will exceed everyone's imagination!

_____

_____

_____

_____

_____

_____

_____

_____

_____

_____

_____

_____

_____

With Your Daughter:

Invite:

Virtue of Mary: Angelic Sweetness: Radiating joy and peace to everyone she encountered

Spend sixty seconds in silence thinking about what Angelic Sweetness means in your life and invite Mary to teach you.

"Come, Holy Spirit. Bring the gift of Angelic Sweetness. Guide our conversation tonight. Blessed Mother, pray for us that we may please God by becoming more like you.

Hail Mary, full of grace the Lord is with you. Blessed are you among women and blessed is the fruit of your womb, Jesus. Holy Mary, Mother of God, pray for us sinners, now and at the hour of our death. Amen"

Discuss:

- ❖ Reflect on your thoughts on Chapter 6. Discuss any topics that may come up.

- ❖ Ask, are you Women in Love with the Lord above all else? Is He the Source and Summit of your life?

❖ When a girl is in love with a boy she makes time for him. Busyness can be quite the distraction from this gentleman in pursuit of your heart. Is it possible that people who think they love God don't really love Him passionately enough to make time for Him? Where do you fit into this point?

❖ When two people falling for one another they do all sorts of things to display their feelings. They do random acts of kindness, give gifts, spend time getting acquainted and say sweet things. What can each of you start doing today to pursue the Lord?

❖ Share your list of attributes you hope to see in her HTB.

❖ Ask her to share write her own list if she is willing. If not that is fine too.

❖ Discuss the differences and similarities. Ask her why she feels certain things are important or unimportant.

Pray:

Pray that the Lord will mold the man He has created for your daughter if she is called to marriage. Pray together that she will grow into the woman the Lord wants to give to this amazing man. Ask most especially that each of you will continue to grow in your pursuit of Love. Ask the Lord to give you the desire to be transformed and radiate as Women in Love.

Novena for the Intercession of Saint Philomena

Saint Philomena! Your life and death gave great glory to the Lord. I rejoice in the ways He has used your witness to inspire generations in their vow of purity. Through this novena I pray that I may come to know you as my sister, my guide, my companion and ally. As I come to you for aid today, I realize that it is not me who discovered you, but you who desire to pray for me. I want to commit myself to purity, but I cannot do it alone. You chose to give your very life for the sake of chastity. Be by my side as I face temptations, pressures and perhaps even ridicule for this decision I have made.

Pray for me particularly, that I may exhibit an unbreakable purity, and strength of soul that is always invincible in every kind of assault. Pray that I may have a generosity to give the Lord every sacrifice. Pray that I will have a love as strong as death for Jesus Christ.

Please pray beside me for these intentions and in addition, if I am called to marriage, I ask for your prayers for my future spouse. Bring these same requests to the heart of our Lord whom you love so much.

God is so good that you gave your blood and your life for Him. God has been so good and so generous to you, and we pray that He will also be so generous to us! He has loved me so much it cost Him His life. He has loved me so much that He has given Himself to live in me in the Eucharist. He loved me so much that He has given me every good and perfect gift in my life. Surely, He will never be deaf to your prayers, nor to mine. Full of confidence, I imitate you as I place all my trust in Him. Amen

FOURTH DAY

Take a few moments in silent prayer to consider that Saint Philomena was a Martyr. This meant she had to suffer... to suffer much... to suffer even unto death. It shows that she showed an invincible patience in these torments. Are suffering and patience found together in you?

Close by praying out loud for any intentions each of you may have.

After meeting with your daughter:

What I learned about my daughter today:

_____

_____

_____

How I am going to pray for my daughter based on this particular conversation:

_____

_____

_____

_____

Prayers I have seen answered since we've begun this journey:

_____

_____

_____

Conversation Seven

Guarding One Another's Soul

- ❖ 1 Thes 4:3-4 This is the will of God, your holiness: that you refrain from immorality, 4that each of you know how to acquire a wife for himself in holiness and honor, 5not in lustful passion as do the Gentiles who do not know God
- ❖ 1 Cor 10:13 No trial has come to you but what is human. God is faithful and will not let you be tried beyond your strength; but with the trial he will also provide a way out, so that you may be able to bear it.
- ❖ Mt 26: 41 Watch and pray that you may not undergo the test. The spirit is willing, but the flesh is weak.
- ❖ 1 Pt 5:8 Be sober and vigilant. Your opponent the devil is prowling around like a roaring lion looking for [someone] to devour.
- ❖ Eph 5: 5 Be sure of this, that no immoral or impure or greedy person, that is, an idolater, has any inheritance in the kingdom of Christ and of God
- ❖ Eph 5:15-18 Watch carefully then how you live, not as foolish persons but as wise, making the most of the opportunity, because the days are evil. Therefore, do not continue in ignorance, but try to understand what is the will of the Lord. And do not get drunk on wine, in which lies debauchery, but be filled with the Spirit

Before Meeting With Your Daughter:

Conversation Seven- Goal: To establish clear guidelines for protecting your daughter's sexuality.

Prepare:

You may ask "Wow- where do I even start with this Chapter?" Begin by rereading the "Further Tips for Talking to Your Daughter About Sexuality" at the beginning of this book.

If you haven't already, pray about sharing your own story with your daughter if you are comfortable. If you waited for marriage, now is a time to affirm what a blessing that has been in your life. If you didn't wait, let God bring a good from it! Our God is **so** amazing that He can use us in spite of ourselves! Remember some of the greatest Heroes of our faith, David, Moses, Saint Paul, Saint Augustine… the list goes on and on. Aren't all of us examples of God bringing a great good out of imperfection?

- ❖ If you decide to share your story be sure to remember the rules of a good faith sharing:
    - o Pray through the story and allow God to show you the ways He was working and present.
    - o Never glorify the sin in any way.
- ❖ Example: "I used to do x, y and z and it was awesome. Those were the days…"
    - o Specifics and details are not necessary; general statements are best. They get the point across without distracting from the message.
    - o Mention the pain and consequences of sin and emphasize the intense glory of God's goodness when we follow His plan!

When you are done with this chapter, congratulate yourself! The door is now open. Your daughter knows exactly where you stand and you have shown her that you feel her body is a treasure. The next time she has a question, she will know that you are willing to find the answer with her. She will know she doesn't have to turn to friends, the internet or magazines for advice.

If your daughter was less than enthusiastic or reluctant to talk, please resist the urge to be discouraged. This is a tough topic, one that may have been difficult for you to breach. That being the case, your daughter may not have the tools, maturity or humility to open up to you. I promise you, teenagers hear much more than they let on. Their image can be so important to them that it forbids them from being themselves. Keep your head up and trudge on, continue showing your daughter that you are in for the long haul. Pray that the Lord will give root to the seeds you have planted and let Him know that you don't necessarily need to see the fruit.

Notes:

With Your Daughter:

Invite:

Virtue of Mary: Surpassing Purity: Having a heart immaculately clean and unstained by sin

Spend sixty seconds in silence thinking about what Surpassing Purity means in your life and invite Mary to teach you.

"Come, Holy Spirit. Bring the gift of Surpassing Purity. Guide our conversation tonight. Blessed Mother, pray for us that we may please God by becoming more like you.

Hail Mary, full of grace the Lord is with you. Blessed are you among women and blessed is the fruit of your womb, Jesus. Holy Mary, Mother of God, pray for us sinners, now and at the hour of our death. Amen"

Discuss:

❖ Since there is so much practical advice in this chapter, I would advise going page by page with your daughter.

❖ Ask her what questions. It may be uncomfortable, but remember, you want her coming to you with those questions, not going elsewhere for answers.

Pray:

Call to mind the request for "Courageous Purity". This kind of purity will not go unrewarded. Pray for a strengthening of your relationship with one another and ask the Lord for more conversations like this one.

Novena for the Intercession of Saint Philomena

Saint Philomena! Your life and death gave great glory to the Lord. I rejoice in the ways He has used your witness to inspire generations in their vow of purity. Through this novena I pray that I may come to know you as my sister, my guide, my companion and ally. As I come to you for aid today, I realize that it is not me who discovered you, but you who desire to pray for me. I want to commit myself to purity, but I cannot do it alone. You chose to give your very life for the sake of chastity. Be by my side as I face temptations, pressures and perhaps even ridicule for this decision I have made.

Pray for me particularly, that I may exhibit an unbreakable purity, and strength of soul that is always invincible in every kind of assault. Pray that I may have a generosity to give the Lord every sacrifice. Pray that I will have a love as strong as death for Jesus Christ.

Please pray beside me for these intentions and in addition, if I am called to marriage, I ask for your prayers for my future spouse. Bring these same requests to the heart of our Lord whom you love so much.

God is so good that you gave your blood and your life for Him. God has been so good and so generous to you, and we pray that He will also be so generous to us! He has loved me so much it cost Him His life. He has loved me so much that He has given Himself to live in me in the Eucharist. He loved me so much that He has given me every good and perfect gift in my life. Surely, He will never be deaf to your prayers, nor to mine. Full of confidence, I imitate you as I place all my trust in Him. Amen

FIFTH DAY

Take a few moments to silently consider that Saint Philomena suffered martyrdom for Jesus Christ. They wanted to wrestle her Faith from her and persuade her to follow the example of the world. What does the devil, the world, the flesh and your own heart want from you on so many occasions that challenge you to be unfaithful? To overcome the desire to be accepted by others, say to yourself from time to time: "It is better to please God than men." Remember Him as your First Love.

Close by praying out loud for any intentions each of you may have.

After meeting with your daughter:

What I learned about my daughter today:

_____

_____

_____

How I am going to pray for my daughter based on this particular conversation:

_____

_____

_____

_____

Prayers I have seen answered since we've begun this journey:

_____

_____

_____

_____

Conversation Eight

Guarding One Another's Body

❖ Rev 2:10b Remain faithful until death, and I will give you the crown of life.

❖ 2 Sm 22:31 God's way is unerring; the LORD's promise is tried and true; he is a shield for all who trust in Him.

❖ Ps 91:14-15 Because he clings to me I will deliver him; because he knows my name I will set him on high. He will call upon me and I will answer; I will be with him in distress; I will deliver him and give him honor.

Before Meeting With Your Daughter:

Conversation Eight- Goal: To have an articulate discussion about the dangers of premarital sex on the physical and spiritual level.

Prepare:

No one likes to talk about Sexually Transmitted Diseases. Be prepared for a few eye rolls and an occasional "Moooom!" As I share in *Woman in Love*, I too struggled with the use of STDs in chastity talks. I wanted to be sure I had the right motivation for sharing this information. Scaring our kids into abstinence isn't the answer, but giving them the tools to make a good choice is.

If you have more questions about HPV, the vaccines or STDs I would recommend www.chastityproject.com as a great resource for further reading.

Notes:

Write any points that you want to bring to your daughter's attention concerning this chapter.

_____

_____

_____

_____

_____

With Your Daughter:

Invite:

Virtue of Mary: Divine Wisdom: Always begging for God's Spirit to guide her

Spend sixty seconds in silence thinking about what Divine Wisdom means in your life and invite Mary to teach you.

"Come, Holy Spirit. Bring the gift of Divine Wisdom. Guide our conversation tonight. Blessed Mother, pray for us that we may please God by becoming more like you.

Hail Mary, full of grace the Lord is with you. Blessed are you among women and blessed is the fruit of your womb, Jesus. Holy Mary, Mother of God, pray for us sinners, now and at the hour of our death. Amen"

Discuss:

- ❖ There is probably no shortage of surprises in this chapter. You should have a lot to discuss.

- ❖ Ask your daughter what she has heard about Sexually Transmitted Diseases from health class, friends and the media.

❖ Do your best to echo the ways you relate to God's sentiments about protecting His daughter.

   o Although we have done a load of affirming up to this point, it never hurts to continue to build up our daughters!

   o Don't forget to be confident that she is listening, and your words of affirmation run deeper than you can ever imagine... even if she doesn't want you to know!

Pray:

Pray in thanksgiving! Praise God for His incredible plan and design! Ask Him to help you live within that design at all times.

Novena for the Intercession of Saint Philomena

Saint Philomena! Your life and death gave great glory to the Lord. I rejoice in the ways He has used your witness to inspire generations in their vow of purity. Through this novena I pray that I may come to know you as my sister, my guide, my companion and ally. As I come to you for aid today, I realize that it is not me who discovered you, but you who desire to pray for me. I want to commit myself to purity, but I cannot do it alone. You chose to give your very life for the sake of chastity. Be by my side as I face temptations, pressures and perhaps even ridicule for this decision I have made.

Pray for me particularly, that I may exhibit an unbreakable purity, and strength of soul that is always invincible in every kind of assault. Pray that I may have a generosity to give the Lord every sacrifice. Pray that I will have a love as strong as death for Jesus Christ.

Please pray beside me for these intentions and in addition, if I am called to marriage, I ask for your prayers for my future spouse. Bring these same requests to the heart of our Lord whom you love so much.

God is so good that you gave your blood and your life for Him. God has been so good and so generous to you, and we pray that He will also be so generous to us! He has loved me so much it cost Him His life. He has loved me so much that He has given Himself to live in me in the Eucharist. He loved me so much that He has given me every good and perfect gift in my life. Surely, He will never be deaf to your prayers, nor to mine. Full of confidence, I imitate you as I place all my trust in Him. Amen

SIXTH DAY

Take some time to silently consider that Saint Philomena did not hesitate. She sacrificed everything, no matter how her blood and her nature raised their voices in protest. Do we find ourselves willing to sacrifice in far less difficult situations? Let us work to please only God, or to please others solely for God's sake.

Close by praying out loud for any intentions each of you may have.

After meeting with your daughter:

What I learned about my daughter today:

_____

_____

_____

How I am going to pray for my daughter based on this particular conversation:

_____

_____

_____

_____

Prayers I have seen answered since we've begun this journey:

_____

_____

_____

_____

Conversation Nine

Modest is Hottest

❖ Rom 13:14 Put on the Lord Jesus Christ, and make no provision for the desires of the flesh.

❖ 1 Cor 6:19-20 Do you not know that your body is a temple of the holy Spirit within you, whom you have from God, and that you are not your own? For you have been purchased at a price. Therefore, glorify God in your body.

❖ Pv 11:22 Like a golden ring in a swine's snout is a beautiful woman without judgment.

❖ Mt 5:28 But I say to you, everyone who looks at a woman with lust has already committed adultery with her in his heart.

Before Meeting With Your Daughter:

Conversation Nine- Goal: To establish a standard for dress that reflects, not distracts, from the dignity of your daughter.

Prepare:

Modesty is often the hardest part to sell when it comes to purity. I find that an important element to success is accountability. It can be very hurtful to have immodest clothing commented on, even by a well-meaning observer. Help your daughter avoid these comments or thoughts. Fight for her reputation and her image. Decide to be a team when it comes to modesty so that you and your daughter can dress like women who are spoken for by your First Love.

Be prepared that this might mean some sacrifices on your part. Weigh the rewards. Your example could help divert the prying eyes of men who may gaze at the body of your little girl. If that means you have to do away with your favorite low-cut top, it would be worth it. Ask the Lord for clarity and courage for both of you!

Notes:

Take some time asking the Lord to convict you on this topic. Ask the Holy Spirit for the right words at the right moments when you approach this touchy topic with your daughter.

_____

_____

_____

_____

With Your Daughter:

Invite:

Virtue of Mary: Lively Faith: Constantly seeking God's will and never settling for complacency

Spend sixty seconds in silence thinking about what Lively Faith means in your life and invite Mary to teach you.

"Come, Holy Spirit. Bring the gift of Lively Faith. Guide our conversation tonight. Blessed Mother, pray for us that we may please God by becoming more like you.

Hail Mary, full of grace the Lord is with you. Blessed are you among women and blessed is the fruit of your womb, Jesus. Holy Mary, Mother of God, pray for us sinners, now and at the hour of our death. Amen"

Discuss:

❖ Talk about Chapter 9 and discuss the sections that stood out to each of you.

❖ Together, come up with your own list of modesty guidelines or use some from the "Your Story" section of Chapter 9.

❖ Agree upon these as a modesty covenant that you and your daughter will hold one another to.

❖ Give **each other** permission to help in this category, so that you alone aren't the modesty police.

❖ Reread the quote at the top of page 108 of *Woman in Love* together. Ask if it is a sacrifice you are both willing to make. Why or why not?

❖ Never ever forget to make it worth it! Ask your daughter if she is willing to offer her sacrifice up for the purity of her future spouse.

Pray:

Pray for the *desire* for modesty. Ask the Lord for more holy men in the world. Pray for the clarity to see what doesn't come naturally.

Novena for the Intercession of Saint Philomena

Saint Philomena! Your life and death gave great glory to the Lord. I rejoice in the ways He has used your witness to inspire generations in their vow of purity. Through this novena I pray that I may come to know you as my sister, my guide, my companion and ally. As I come to you for aid today, I realize that it is not me who discovered you, but you who desire to pray for me. I want to commit myself to purity, but I cannot do it alone. You chose to give your very life for the sake of chastity. Be by my side as I face temptations, pressures and perhaps even ridicule for this decision I have made.

Pray for me particularly, that I may exhibit an unbreakable purity, and strength of soul that is always invincible in every kind of assault. Pray that I may have a generosity to give the Lord every sacrifice. Pray that I will have a love as strong as death for Jesus Christ.

Please pray beside me for these intentions and in addition, if I am called to marriage, I ask for your prayers for my future spouse. Bring these same requests to the heart of our Lord whom you love so much.

God is so good that you gave your blood and your life for Him. God has been so good and so generous to you, and we pray that He will also be so generous to us! He has loved me so much it cost Him His life. He has loved me so much that He has given Himself to live in me in the Eucharist. He loved me so much that He has given me every good and perfect gift in my life. Surely, He will never be deaf to your prayers, nor to mine. Full of confidence, I imitate you as I place all my trust in Him. Amen

SEVENTH DAY

Take a few moments in silence to consider that Saint Philomena, in dying for Jesus Christ, had to endure the jeers, the sarcasms, the outrages of her persecutors, of her executioners and of the majority of the witnesses to her torture. She was nonetheless generous, nonetheless constant and nonetheless joyous in the public confession of her faith. Do not allow your heart to be changed if abrupt words are spoken to you, or rough, biting and offensive words are hurled at you. Fear nothing… Follow out your road… It is leading straight to eternal glory.

Close by praying out loud for any intentions each of you may have.

After meeting with your daughter:

What I learned about my daughter today:

_____

_____

_____

How I am going to pray for my daughter based on this particular conversation:

_____

_____

_____

_____

Prayers I have seen answered since we've begun this journey:

_____

_____

_____

_____

Conversation Ten

Total Gift of Self

❖ Genesis 1:28a God blessed them and God said to them: Be fertile and multiply; fill the earth and subdue it.

❖ Genesis 9:1,7 God blessed Noah and his sons and said to them: Be fertile and multiply and fill the earth...Be fertile, then, and multiply; abound on earth and subdue it.

❖ Genesis 38:8-10 Then Judah said to Onan, "Have intercourse with your brother's wife, in fulfillment of your duty as brother-in-law, and thus preserve your brother's line." Onan, however, knew that the offspring would not be his; so whenever he had intercourse with his brother's wife, he wasted his seed on the ground, to avoid giving offspring to his brother. What he did greatly offended the LORD, and the LORD took his life too.

Before Meeting With Your Daughter

Conversation Ten- Goal: To help this particular child understand that children are joy, and that she is an example of this truth.

Prepare:

Recall the way you felt when you first laid eyes on your daughter. After having her baby, a friend of mine once said that she felt like her heart worked for the first time. From the instant of your own conception, God desired to use your daughter to reveal Himself to you. Reflect on the ways that children make us holier. Think about the ways you have been drawn out of yourself. Remember the times you stumbled to a crib in the middle of the night expecting to be annoyed at its inhabitant only to experience the melting of your heart when you saw your daughter's face. He knew you would experience generosity and overwhelming affection as well as brokenheartedness and pain. He wants to use her to show you His deep, passionate, wild love for **you**!

When we are married the priest asks, "Will you accept children lovingly from the Lord?" Children are a way that the Lord makes our love for each other and for Him visible. The issue of contraception is a tough one. You may personally struggle with this topic, and it is okay to be honest about that. As always, simply pray that the Lord will stretch and challenge you with gentleness on this journey. The focus of this discussion with your daughter is ensuring that she knows that sex and babies go together. There has been a break of this notion in our culture and the repercussions are frightening. Use your daughter's presence in your life as a witness of the beauty of openness to life.

In recent workshops I have been shocked at how little teenage girls know about how their fertility cycle and reproductive organs work. I have heard many questions about eggs, uterine lining and even menopause that I was previously confident that these young women already knew. My theory is that when a young girl is given the talk regarding the "Birds and the Bees" that they make be a tad overwhelmed with this earth shattering information. Certain facts stick and perhaps others may be lost in the absorption of it all. It may be true that some girls are too nervous to address their questions about their bodies. Tonight you will open a door that might lead to questions regarding this topic. You may want to brush up yourself, but don't feel the pressure to know all the answers. Assure your daughter that you will find the information for her.

Again, this will probably be uncomfortable. However, don't forget that you want to be her source of information on these sensitive topics! Remember your mission statement. What are you doing this? What do you hope to accomplish?

If you have more questions on the Church's teachings on contraception and how to be faithful to them, please check out these resources:

- ❖ **Humanae Vitae:** http://www.scborromeo.org/docs/humanae_vitae.pdf Papal Encyclical of Pope Paul VI.
- ❖ **The Couple to Couple League:** www.ccli.org A leading organization for the widely used Sympto-Thermal method of Natural Family Planning.
- ❖ **The Creighton Model:** www.creightonmodel.com The site from the founders of the incredible Napro-Technology system of NFP. Creighton is also a great option for those who have issues with their cycle and desire a natural approach to cramping, irregular cycles and infertility.
- ❖ **1 Flesh:** www.1flesh.org. This is a great resource for a secular approach to this topic.

Notes:

Make some notes regarding your thoughts on this important topic. Include any points that you would like to address with your daughter in regards to her fertility cycle in general.

_____

_____

_____

_____

_____

_____

_____

_____

_____

_____

_____

_____

_____

With Your Daughter

Invite:

Virtue of Mary: **Universal Mortification:** Seeking to lay down her life and her will at every moment

Spend sixty seconds in silence thinking about what Universal Mortification means in your life and invite Mary to teach you.

"Come, Holy Spirit. Bring the gift of Universal Mortification. Guide our conversation tonight. Blessed Mother, pray for us that we may please God by becoming more like you.

Hail Mary, full of grace the Lord is with you. Blessed are you among women and blessed is the fruit of your womb, Jesus. Holy Mary, Mother of God, pray for us sinners, now and at the hour of our death. Amen"

Discuss:

- ❖ Talk about Chapter 10 and discuss the sections that stood out to each of you.
- ❖ Ask what questions your daughter has regarding her own cycle. This may include what happens during her cycle, cramping or other physical signs that may not seem normal, or specifics on what happens during a pregnancy etc.

❖ Read John 10:10 together. Discuss the way it relates to the topic of contraception.

❖ Tell her the story of her birth (even if she has heard it a million times).

❖ Share your reflections from the *Prepare* section regarding the blessing she is.

❖ Ask what she is most excited about when she pictures herself as a mother.

❖ What is she most nervous about?

❖ Tell her the reasons you know she will be a blessing to her future children.

Pray:

You want the world for your daughter and pray tonight that the Lord will give it all to her. Pray that He will reveal any impediments to the life He has in store for her.

Novena for the Intercession of Saint Philomena

Saint Philomena! Your life and death gave great glory to the Lord. I rejoice in the ways He has used your witness to inspire generations in their vow of purity. Through this novena I pray that I may come to know you as my sister, my guide, my companion and ally. As I come to you for aid today, I realize that it is not me who discovered you, but you who desire to pray for me. I want to commit myself to purity, but I cannot do it alone. You chose to give your very life for the sake of chastity. Be by my side as I face temptations, pressures and perhaps even ridicule for this decision I have made.

Pray for me particularly, that I may exhibit an unbreakable purity, and strength of soul that is always invincible in every kind of assault. Pray that I may have a generosity to give the Lord every sacrifice. Pray that I will have a love as strong as death for Jesus Christ.

Please pray beside me for these intentions and in addition, if I am called to marriage, I ask for your prayers for my future spouse. Bring these same requests to the heart of our Lord whom you love so much.

God is so good that you gave your blood and your life for Him. God has been so good and so generous to you, and we pray that He will also be so generous to us! He has loved me so much it cost Him His life. He has loved me so much that He has given Himself to live in me in the Eucharist. He loved me so much that He has given me every good and perfect gift in my life. Surely, He will never be deaf to your prayers, nor to mine. Full of confidence, I imitate you as I place all my trust in Him. Amen

EIGHTH DAY

Silently consider that when Saint Philomena died, for love of Jesus Christ, to all the things of the world, she entered into the joy of eternal life. Her motivation was to protect the heart of her First Love. She kept her eyes fixed on Heaven. Are these the thoughts which I try to have when I find myself confronted with some sacrifice? Ask for eyes that will see the face of the Lord at all moments and in every trial.

Close by praying out loud for any intentions each of you may have.

After meeting with your daughter:

What I learned about my daughter today:

_____

_____

_____

How I am going to pray for my daughter based on this particular conversation:

_____

_____

_____

_____

Prayers I have seen answered since we've begun this journey:

_____

_____

_____

_____

Conversation Eleven

Transforming Mercy

❖ Ps 145:8 The LORD is gracious and merciful, slow to anger and
abounding in mercy.

❖ James 5:11 Indeed we call blessed those who have persevered. You
have heard of the perseverance of Job, and you have seen the
purpose of the Lord, because "the Lord is compassionate and
merciful.

❖ Prv 29:15 If we acknowledge our sins, he is faithful and just and will
forgive our sins and cleanse us from every wrongdoing.

❖ Gal 5:1 For freedom Christ set us free; so stand firm and do not
submit again to the yoke of slavery.

Before Meeting With Your Daughter

Conversation Eleven- Goal: To provide an atmosphere of mercy in your home and give an opportunity for reconciliation of past hurts.

Prepare:

Of course you fight with you daughter… sometimes it seems like you fight all the time. One of the many duties of parenthood is to be a living witness of the mercy of God. You will show your daughter what both mercy and justice look like in the big things and in the little ones. Consider using this night as an opportunity to talk about your relationship and some ways you can work on it together. This will only be possible if you feel that you can avoid feeling defensive and getting angry. This night is about finding the best way that you can communicate with your daughter, not the other way around. The idea isn't to turn a discussion of reconciliation into a blow out! If you don't feel you can remain calm and focused then please avoid the following approach.

Here are a few pointers to keep it from going south.

❖ If she has some feelings that you feel are unfounded i.e. "You never listen," "You don't appreciate me," "nothing is ever good enough," (can you tell I've worked with teenagers?) don't react defensively. Sometimes teens are like wild animals. One has to approach them with caution until they see you aren't a threat. While these feelings may have <u>no</u> facts to support them, the *feelings* themselves are **real** nonetheless. Affirm your daughter and *gulp* ask her how you can do better.

❖ Remember, this conversation is about improving your communication skills and helping you to be a witness of mercy. This is a time to show her that you support her, not a time to bring up your own gripes.

❖ Don't forget your mission statement! Why are you doing this? Keep this at the forefront of this entire conversation.

❖ When I find myself in tough conversations I often repeat, "Come, Holy Spirit" over and over in my mind. I can tell you that when we are open and listening He tends to deliver.

❖ Anticipate some challenges you may have today. Pray for the gifts of Wisdom and Counsel that you received in your Confirmation to come to your aid.

❖ End the conversation with an affirmation of love. Then follow through. This doesn't mean you let her walk all over you, but it does mean that then next time things get hairy between the two of you, you can show her that you listened. Be sure and point out you efforts to her so she can recognize and appreciate them.

Notes:

_____

_____

_____

_____

_____

_____

_____

_____

_____

_____

_____

_____

_____

_____

With Your Daughter

Invite:

Virtue of Mary: Constant Mental Prayer: Always being aware of God's presence

Spend sixty seconds in silence thinking about what Constant Mental Prayer means in your life and invite Mary to teach you.

"Come, Holy Spirit. Bring the gift of Constant Mental Prayer. Guide our conversation tonight. Blessed Mother, pray for us that we may please God by becoming more like you.

Hail Mary, full of grace the Lord is with you. Blessed are you among women and blessed is the fruit of your womb, Jesus. Holy Mary, Mother of God, pray for us sinners, now and at the hour of our death. Amen"

Discuss:

❖ Talk about Chapter 11 and discuss the sections that stood out to each of you.

❖ Ask your daughter if she has problems accepting God's forgiveness or forgiving herself. Ask her to explain.

❖ Invite her to share her feelings about forgiving her Husband-To-Be if he has made mistakes.

❖ Tell your daughter that you want to help reveal God's mercy to her. Ask how you can best approach her when you are disappointed in her to keep her from feeling defensive.

❖ Ask her where she wants to find healing in the relationship between the two of you.

❖ Thank her for her honesty and affirm her in the things she may be feeling.

Pray:

Pray together that God will show you both how to be merciful, sacrificial and selfless in your relationship with one another.

Novena for the Intercession of Saint Philomena- Final Day

Saint Philomena! Your life and death gave great glory to the Lord. I rejoice in the ways He has used your witness to inspire generations in their vow of purity. Through this novena I pray that I may come to know you as my sister, my guide, my companion and ally. As I come to you for aid today, I realize that it is not me who discovered you, but you who desire to pray for me. I want to commit myself to purity, but I cannot do it alone. You chose to give your very life for the sake of chastity. Be by my side as I face temptations, pressures and perhaps even ridicule for this decision I have made.

Pray for me particularly, that I may exhibit an unbreakable purity, and strength of soul that is always invincible in every kind of assault. Pray that I may have a generosity to give the Lord every sacrifice. Pray that I will have a love as strong as death for Jesus Christ.

Please pray beside me for these intentions and in addition, if I am called to marriage, I ask for your prayers for my future spouse. Bring these same requests to the heart of our Lord whom you love so much.

God is so good that you gave your blood and your life for Him. God has been so good and so generous to you, and we pray that He will also be so generous to us! He has loved me so much it cost Him His life. He has loved me so much that He has given Himself to live in me in the Eucharist. He loved me so much that He has given me every good and perfect gift in my life. Surely, He will never be deaf to your prayers, nor to mine. Full of confidence, I imitate you as I place all my trust in Him. Amen

NINTH DAY

Silently consider that Saint Philomena, having sacrificed everything in this world for Jesus Christ, received back from Him more than the hundredfold of what she had given! God fulfills His every promise. If only we maintained our promises to Him with the same fidelity! But when we deprive Him of His glory, do we not perhaps deprive ourselves? The Lord wants to give you His mercy and manifest His glory in you! Have courage, therefore to be faithful in order that God may be faithful with you.

Close by praying out loud for any intentions each of you may have.

After meeting with your daughter:

What I learned about my daughter today:

_____

_____

_____

How I am going to pray for my daughter based on this particular conversation:

_____

_____

_____

_____

Prayers I have seen answered since we've begun this journey:

_____

_____

_____

_____

Conversation Twelve and Epilogue

Your Reason

* Mk 9:23 Jesus said to him, "'If you can!' Everything is possible to one who has faith."

* 2 Tim 2:5 Similarly, an athlete cannot receive the winner's crown except by competing according to the rules.

* Phil 4:13 I have the strength for everything through him who empowers me.

* James 1:12 Blessed is the man who perseveres in temptation, for when he has been proved he will receive the crown of life that he promised to those who love him.

* Ex 19:5 Now, if you obey me completely and keep my covenant, you will be my treasured possession among all peoples, though all the earth is mine.

Before Meeting With Your Daughter

Conversation Twelve- Goal: To solidify this experience as a life change and resolution for the future.

Prepare:

Here it is! The completion! Plan something special for your daughter tonight. You may decide on a special dinner date, Mass and Adoration or a small outing. This should include you, your daughter and, if possible, her father. If possible allow her dad to take the lead this evening. Generally speaking, most families decide that mom will handle the sexuality discussion with the girls of the family and dad will talk to the boys. While this is definitely the more comfortable option, I feel strongly that it is important for each parent to talk to each child together about the importance of purity. There is something powerful about a father showing his daughter that he is the first man to desire her purity. To make things flow a little easier, prior to the date, each parent can write a letter explaining why her purity is important to you.

This moment will be the climax of this entire endeavor. The highlight should be a token of your commitment to your daughter and God's Will for her life. I would highly recommend choosing a chastity ring to present to her. A chastity ring is an incredible reminder of the hope you have for your daughter's future. It is meant to be worn on her ring finger of her left hand until it is replaced by another. On a side note, regarding this ring, I can share my personal experience. For my 18th birthday, my best friends bought me a chastity ring. One night a college boy was preparing to approach me to ask for my number. He asked an acquaintance if I was engaged because he noticed my ring. She explained its significance. He responded that in it should be called an "eternal virginity ring" instead of a purity ring. Needless to say he didn't ask for my digits, and also needless to say, I was plenty glad he didn't. If you'd like, you can think of this ring as a creep repellent as well. You can find purity rings at most

Christian bookstores. They are very, very reasonably priced. If you can't find one, there are some great options online.

Before the big day I would suggest doing a little bit of research of those who have gone before you. For those of you who haven't seen it already, please drop everything right now and go rent the movie "Courageous". There is a BEAUTIFUL scene at the end of the film where a father gives his daughter a similar ring. Make sure you have tissues handy.

As you present the ring to your daughter, think about the proposal that will likely replace it one day. Consider the promise you intend to make to your daughter- that, if she allows you, you will do everything you can to walk with her in her discernment of the person God has in store for her. Ask her for permission to help her guard the heart you care so deeply for. You will explain this day that your love is big enough to encompass her mistakes and that you are always here for her.

In my ministry I have the incredible blessing to witness stories of young women who have championed in purity. One of these such opportunities is the Woman In Love Mother Daughter Purity Retreat, which ends with a purity ring ceremony similar to what you will experience. I want to let a few of the girls who have attended tell you in their own words what their parent's involvement meant to them. Both girls have since graduated from college and have not only kept their promise to purity, but have grown to be incredibly amazing young women who are so in love in love with the Lord:

"Emerging from the Chapel on the morning of my first purity retreat, I was suddenly surprised to see a familiar face, gently beckoning me towards her. The retreat had been so touching already; yet, it continued to get even better. After I had told her a little about the retreat, my mother began to explain why she was there. Although I can't remember her exact words, she conveyed to me her desire for my purity. Of all the things my mother expects of me, this is probably the most touching. I had learned from the night before that at the core of a pure heart is a profound encounter with the Divine, for as Jesus said: "Blessed are the pure of heart, for they shall see God." So, by hearing my mother say she wanted me to be pure, meant to me that she also wanted me to be holy. Her voicing this desire instantly fueled my flame a little more. She also gave me a ring, which was an external sign of her confidence in my ability to become a woman of God. I know as daughters we naturally look to our mothers to learn what it means to be a woman and also what it means to be beautiful. My mom assured me that she believed I

*could be pure, that I could be holy, and that I was beautiful. This **empowered** me. We don't have a lovey-dovey, perfect relationship, but I can tell you that this little exchange on the pew is one I will never be able to forget. For in this moment, my mother gave me more than a ring; she opened her heart and demonstrated to me how purity and holiness were intricately related to true beauty and true femininity. And her desire became my desire; it was the perfect conviction that I needed to pursue the vision of a Woman in Love."*

- Shannon K.

"Walking into the church and seeing both of my parents waiting for me was one of the biggest surprises of the sleepover. They were aware that I was on the way to making my faith my own and because of this they recognized the importance of showing me that they would walk beside me. My father always inspired me through the ways he worked so hard to support my five siblings and me. Due to an extensive work schedule, there were very few times he was able to make it to church with us as a family. The fact that my dad was there with my mom made me feel so loved.

When I met them in the pew and my mom started to read the letter that they had both taken time to write for me, I couldn't help but feel so empowered to really strive to keep that promise to be a woman who waited. I knew this was something important. I felt such strength and love in that moment. It was really one of those times where I can look back and see God and the way He has been ever present in my life. The love, support and strength that I felt from my parents that day was a true reflection of what my Heavenly Father was and always is feeling for me.

Several years later, my father passed away. This fact has made this memory even more precious to me. It kills me to think that he won't be there to physically walk me down the aisle on my wedding day. However, when I think about it, I find much comfort in knowing that he will have helped me get down the aisle in the first place. He, along with my mother, and all that I have learned about being a Woman In Love, has helped me to see the importance of waiting. Waiting and remaining pure is the beginning of my future commitment to the man I will one day marry. My promise that day to my mother and father was my first step down the aisle. It is priceless to know that both my earthly father and Heavenly Father were there with me, holding my hand and guiding me with that first step."

-Mo B.

Notes:

Plan your evening and envision the way you hope it will go! Ask yourself, "why do I hope she waits?" Read the "Discuss" section below and outline your letter here.

_____

_____

_____

_____

_____

_____

_____

_____

_____

_____

_____

_____

Together With Your Daughter

Invite:

Virtue of Mary: Heroic Patience: Always trusting that God was on the move; having more faith in His plans than her own

Spend sixty seconds in silence thinking about what Heroic Patience means in your life and invite Mary to teach you.

"Come, Holy Spirit. Bring the gift of Heroic Patience. Guide our conversation tonight. Blessed Mother, pray for us that we may please God by becoming more like you.

Hail Mary, full of grace the Lord is with you. Blessed are you among women and blessed is the fruit of your womb, Jesus. Holy Mary, Mother of God, pray for us sinners, now and at the hour of our death. Amen"

Discuss:

❖ Reflect as a family on the virtue of Heroic Patience. What makes this difficult? What are the rewards?

❖ Open the discussion by reading the letters prepared for your daughter.

❖ The conclusion of *Woman in Love* is centered on finding Christ as "Your Reason" for purity. Express your desires for your daughter to keep her eyes on the prize.

❖ As you present the ring to your daughter, think about the proposal that will likely replace it one day. Make a promise to your daughter that, if she allows you, you will do everything you can to walk with her in her discernment of the person God has in store for her. Ask her for permission to help her guard the heart you care so deeply for. If she replies "yes", place the ring on her finger.

❖ Explain that your love is big enough to encompass her mistakes and that you are always here for her. Thank her for trusting you and for the opportunity to walk this road together.

Pray:

Pray with your daughter tonight, but be sure she knows that this is only the beginning. Explain that you are climbing in those trenches with her and she doesn't have to be alone. You are going to war with her for her purity and her HTB's.

After meeting with your daughter:

What I learned about my daughter today:

_____

_____

_____

How I am going to pray for my daughter based on this particular conversation:

_____

_____

_____

_____

Prayers I have seen answered since we've begun this journey:

_____

_____

_____

_____

Keep the Conversation Going...

Whew! You did it! Praise Him!

Remember, this is the beginning, not an ending! Hopefully you will have many conversations with your daughter in the years to come. Even more importantly, don't forget to hit your knees for her and her vocation!

Here are some suggestions for future communications:

1. Remember that candle I suggested to be lit during each conversation regarding *Woman In Love*? Remind your daughter of the "secret signal." Invite her to bring the candle out when she needs to talk to you privately and make sure that you follow through on that promise within a reasonable time frame. Continue to light the candle when you meet together.

2. Often times it is easier to express our feelings through writing than verbalizing. Try using a shared mother/daughter journal. This activity involves a single notebook that you place on one another's bed. She can write letters or questions to you about anything she wants and then move it to your bed when she is finished. You can then reciprocate. Depending on your personalities, this may be the a great way to stay connected.

3. In youth ministry we often use a tactic called a "Pulse Check." In this practice I would consciously ask teens during a retreat or conference to share what was happening in their heart. In daily life, a pulse check may happen with an e-mail, phone call or text to a random teen during the week asking them how they were doing. Be sure to check in on your daughter's heart and ask her at least once a week how you can pray for her.

Stay on Your Knees, Mama!

Below are some specific ways you can pray for all your children:

1. One of my favorite prayers for my daughter is inspired by the great St. Therese. Upon her death, her confessor declared that he believed that St. Therese had never committed a serious sin in her entire life. When reading her journals after her death, it was found that St. Therese stated that she believed that the Lord had removed the "stones from in front of her apple cart." This meant that St. Therese believe that God protected her from opportunities to stumble in her moral life. The Lord's mercy preceded Therese in her temptations. I often ask our Father for mercy that is poured out in front of my children in their path of decision making.

    Additionally, as a mother, I ask the Lord to reveal to me the ways that I may remove the stumbling blocks from my children's path. In ancient times, the Mass was held within the home and it was dubbed the "Domestic Church." Our homes are still called to be thus, and we s parents have the responsibility to maintain their sanctity. Take for example the image of Notre Dame in Paris. It is known for its grotesque gargoyles carved in its exterior. Their presence is mean to discourage evil from the property but also to remind us of the wickedness of the world. Within its walls however, we find beauty, peace and sanctity. So it should be with our homes. We must do our best to keep the evil on the outside so that our homes can be trusted as a refuge. Ask the Lord often, and at every stage of your children's lives, to make you aware of the ways that you can help remove temptations from your home and the situations in which you allow your children to enter.

2.   You read about the "Yes Prayer" in Chapter Four of *Woman In Love*. It is so beneficial for us to continually put every aspect of our lives into the hands of the Lord. Moreover, consider praying the "Yes Prayer" each day for your children as well. Tell the Lord that you want to give in to His every Will for their lives, and do so on a daily basis!

3.   One evening, while on the phone with my sister-in-law we got to talking about our own experiences of chastity in our lives. Stephanie was absolutely convicted in her love for purity at a young age and resolved to save her heart and body for her future husband. Due to her passion on the topic, she expressed to me that she wished she could be proactive in molding the same values in her own daughter. She joked that she would like to have a purity talk with her then two year old. While divulging her feelings of temporary helplessness, we started talking about the very St. Philomena that you and your daughter implored for intercession in this very book! St. Philomena is not only the Patroness of Purity for the Twenty-Frist Century, but she is also the Patroness of the Living Rosary. The Living Rosary is classified as one decade per day united to thousands of other people who are committed to a single daily decade. Stephanie and I decided that this practice was more than reasonable and extremely attainable! We have committed to pray our daily decade for our own children, nieces, nephews and godchildren.

Below you will find the specific intentions that I pray for each Hail Mary in the Mother's Decade. My desire for these particular requests pierces my heart as I envision each of these children that I love so deeply! I know that if you give it a try, you too will feel the intense power of these prayers!

The Mother's Decade

1. For the purity of mind for my children.
2. For the purity of body for my children.
3. For the purity of heart and soul for my children.
4. For the purity of intention for my children.
5. For my children's future spouses, whether this be a person or the church.
6. For mercy that precedes my children in their temptations.
7. For my children to have utter confidence in the overwhelming mercy of God.
8. For my children to have the desire to desire God's Will.
9. For my children to have the clarity to see and the courage to do God's Will.
10. For my children to have hearts on fire with love for the Lord.

Wait. Trust. Cling to the Cross...

They say that having a child is making a decision to allow your heart to walk around outside your body. It is one of the most vulnerable forms of love. The Lord chose to make His children with the gift of Free Will. In doing so, He gave us the ability to run to or from Him and to do either by our own choice. This journey will not guarantee that your child will choose the path you hope for her. It will, however, give you insight into the vulnerable heart of our Lord. Now it time to wait, to trust and to cling to the Cross.

The Blessed Mother watched as her Son was beaten, tormented, mocked and killed. She will hold you in the same mothering arms that cradled our Lord both after His birth and His death. In fact, she has done so for your entire life. Follow in her footsteps; she is always walking directly behind the Lord.

Know that God will never be outdone is generosity. When you surrender the most precious part of your life to Him, He will answer beyond your dreams.

...he world needs more mothers who are willing to invest in their children in the way you have done through this journey. My gratitude for your faithfulness is difficult to express, so instead I echo the words of John Paul II:

Thank you, women who are mothers! You have sheltered human beings within yourselves in a unique experience of joy and travail. This experiences makes you become God's own smile upon the newborn child, the one who guides you child's first steps, who helps it to grow, and who is the anchor as the child makes it's way along the journey of live.

John Paul II, Letter to Women, 1995

End Notes:

[i] http://voices.washingtonpost.com/answer-sheet/high-school/a-grinding-problem-with-school.html

[ii] www.crisisconnectioninc.org/teens/media influence on youth.htm

[iii] American Academy Of Pediatrics. Committee On Public Education, American Academy of Child and Adolescent Psychiatry (January 2001). "Sexuality, Contraception, and the Media". *Pediatrics* **107** (1): 191–1994. doi:10.1542/peds.107.1.191. PMID 11134460. http://aappolicy.aappublications.org/cgi/content/full/pediatrics;107/1/191.

[iv] Victor C. Strasburger, MD (2005). "Adolescents, Sex, and the Media: Ooooo, Baby, Baby – a Q & A". *Adolesc Med* **16** (2): 269–288. doi:10.1016/j.admecli.2005.02.009. PMID 16111618.

[v] Jennifer Stevens Aubrey (2004). "Sex and Punishment: An Examination of Sexual Consequences and the Sexual Double Standard in Teen Programming". *Sex Roles* **50** (7–8): 505–514. doi:10.1023/B:SERS.0000023070.87195.07.